J 636.8 PRA
Prap, Lila
Cat whys

082014

Lila Prap
cat Whys

Dear knowledge seekers! Do you have a furry little friend who walks on all fours and meows? You just might, since cats are very popular creatures that many people welcome into their homes as one of the family.

People have been befriending cats for thousands of years, since they realized that cats help keep mice away. In some countries cats were even worshipped as divine. The golden era of the veneration of cats ended in the Middle Ages, when some began to believe that cats were the devil's helpers. Even today in some countries people believe it's unlucky if a black cat crosses your path. Thankfully, these days most people appreciate cats as cute creatures that delight their masters with their playfulness and feline friendship. If you are interested in why your cat behaves the way it does, then take a look at how these mice explain it. If their answers do not satisfy you, then read the expert's comment on each page.

Copyright © 2013 by Mladinska knjiga Založba, d.d., Ljubljana, Slovenia.
First published in 2013 under the title Mačji Zakaji by Mladinska Knjiga Založba, d.d., Ljubljana, Slovenia.
English translation copyright © 2014 by NorthSouth Books, Inc., New York 10016.

First published in the United States, Great Britain, Canada, Australia, and New Zealand in 2014 by NorthSouth Books, Inc.,
an imprint of NordSüd Verlag AG, CH-8005 Zürich, Switzerland.

Distributed in the United States by NorthSouth Books, Inc., New York 10016.
Library of Congress Cataloging-in-Publication Data is available.
ISBN: 978-0-7358-4125-3 (trade edition)
1 3 5 7 9 • 10 8 6 4 2
Printed in China by Toppan Leefung Packaging and Printing (Dongguan) Co., Ltd., Dongguan, P.R.C., March 2014.

www.northsouth.com

Lila Prap

Cat Whys

North
South

Why don't cats obey?

Sit! Get up! Go away!

I know this one! A long time ago, cats were the most obedient creatures the world had seen. Sit, get up, paw, roll over, bring the newspaper . . . they did everything. That was back when they were competing with dogs to win people's affection. But it didn't work. People said, "Cats are better behaved, but dogs look at us so faithfully." This infuriated the cats! "Now, on top of rolling over and fetching, they want us to look at them faithfully!" said the cats. "Well, they can get lost!" From that day onward cats have not listened to people's orders. The only command they obey, if they feel like it, is of course "Puss, come and eat!"

Cats used to obey?! Nonsense! We all know they're too dumb to be told anything.

If you expect a cat to obey your commands like a dog, you've got another think coming. Dogs have inherited from their wolf ancestors the readiness to faithfully follow their leaders. Cats, descended from wild cats, are used to independent thinking, both when hunting and deciding who they will socialize with.

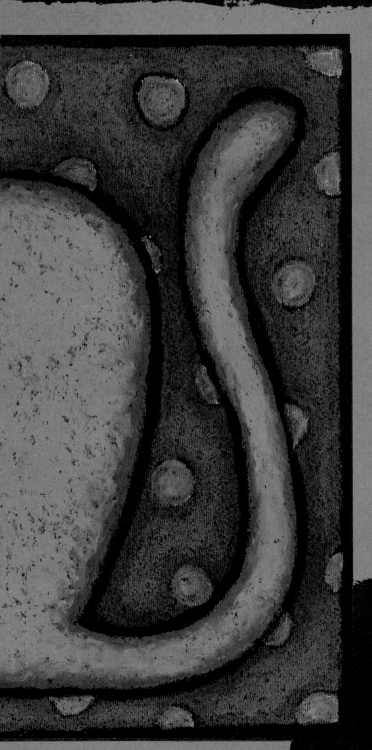

⊤ails?

It's like this. On a farm there lived a cat and a dog. The cat always went around with its tail held high in the air showing off, and this got on the dog's nerves. "Why do you hold your tail up like an antenna? You'll poke my eye out!" the dog said angrily one day. "Can't you wag it a bit when I go past, like you're pleased to see me?" "What do you want me to do?" replied the cat with a yawn. "Wag that antenna of yours a bit! Show that you're aware of others, not just yourself!" said the dog. "Ha! You're going to teach me what to do with my tail!" shouted the cat, waving its tail so that hairs went flying in the air. "Hopeless!" said the dog, trotting away. Even today, cats have still not learned to wag their tails normally.

As I said, you can't tell cats anything. If you could, there would be cat schools as well as dog schools

By waving its tail a cat is trying to say something. But what it is saying is slightly different from dogs. When a cat waves its tail quickly from side to side, it means it is angry, whereas a dog usually does that when it is happy. A cat shows it is happy by holding its tail up high or slightly bent over.

Why do cats hunt mice?

Let me explain! In the beginning, *mice* hunted cats. They waited in their holes, and when they saw a cat . . . they jumped on it, threw it in the air, and tickled it so much that it almost died laughing. "You've gotta learn to laugh!" said the mice. But the cats did not find this funny. "Our fur is dirty now," grumbled the worst-tempered ones. "It would be better if we threw you in the air and tickled you!" said the cats, throwing the mice in the air and scratching them with their long claws.

"They want to kill us! This is no joke!" squeaked the mice who managed to escape the cats' claws.

You see? Cats hunt mice to show them what a real laugh is.

Oh, come on! Cats hunt mice to check if they are real or whether they are seeing things.

Although cats have lived with people for thousands of years, they still have a strong hunting instinct. Even if they are full, they'll chase after every small creature that crosses their path. Cats are extremely patient when hunting. They can wait for hours in front of a mouse hole. They like to bring any mouse they catch to show their owner.

Why do cats' teeth

chatter?

Once upon a time a cat decided it would learn to fly. "If some mice managed to grow wings and change into bats, so will I! I will be the first cat-bat!" It climbed up the tallest tree and looked down. "Hmm, I need some tips about flying," it said after a while to the birds on the next branch. "Tips?" chirped the birds. "You just have to try. If you don't try, you'll never know whether you can fly or not!" The cat spread its paws, lifted its tail, and flew—or rather, it tried to fly. In fact, it dropped like a rock and broke its teeth. "You lying mob of birds! I'll get you!" it yelled, trying to make its teeth chatter. It couldn't because its teeth were broken, but it taught all its kittens to make their teeth chatter whenever they saw a bird.

Cats' teeth chatter because they're afraid that one of the birds or squirrels watching them will fall from the tree!

Cats have inherited the habit of moving their jaws at the sight of birds or squirrels from their wild ancestors, who use a similar jaw movement when applying a deadly bite to the neck of a small animal. Whether they are chattering from frustration that they cannot reach their victims or in order to attract their attention has not been determined.

Why do cats purr?

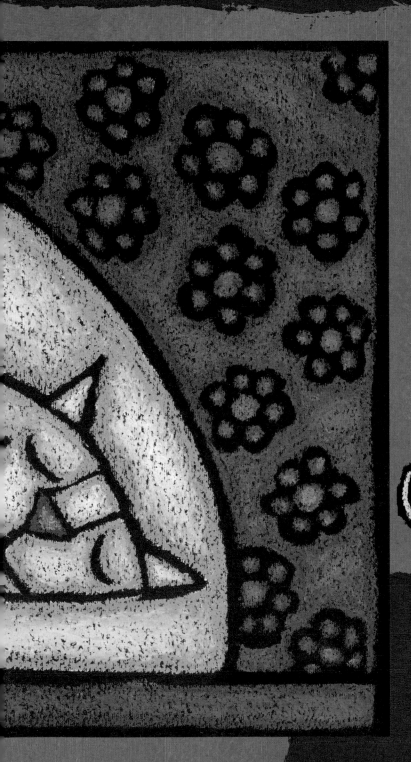

In a castle there lived a cat princess who snored terribly. Suitors stayed well clear of this snoring princess. "I'm not sleeping next to that chain saw, even if they offer me three such kingdoms!" said the last suitor before they threw him out. One day the princess's mother thought, *Our princess is not snoring, but in her dreams she's using a sewing machine to make a beautiful dress.* Since then she had lots of suitors, and all refined cats say they are purring rather than snoring.

That's pathetic! They're growling in their sleep because they can't catch all the mice in the house.

Well, as far as I know, they have a built-in fan to cool them when they get overheated.

Cats' purring is a way of communicating. Cats purr when they are satisfied, but also when they are feeling stressed or frightened. If they feel threatened, their purring says that they do not want to fight.

why can't cats climb

down from trees?

There was once a king who had a tree in his garden that reached into the sky. And because he had read somewhere that golden pears grow on such trees, each day he ordered one of his subjects to climb the tree and bring him one. "If you come down empty-handed, you'll lose your head!" he warned each of them.

And that is what happened, for there were no golden pears on the king's tree. When the king had run out of subjects, he had only his cat left. "Go and get me a golden pear. And don't come down without one!" he ordered the cat. The cat was not keen to lose its head, so it simply stayed up in the tree.

What nonsense—kings and golden pears! They can't get down because they can't fly. Weren't you listening earlier?

It's very easy for cats, whose claws bend backward, to grip the surface on the way up. On the way down they can only grab on if they move backward, which is much more difficult.

Why do cats sharpen

their claws?

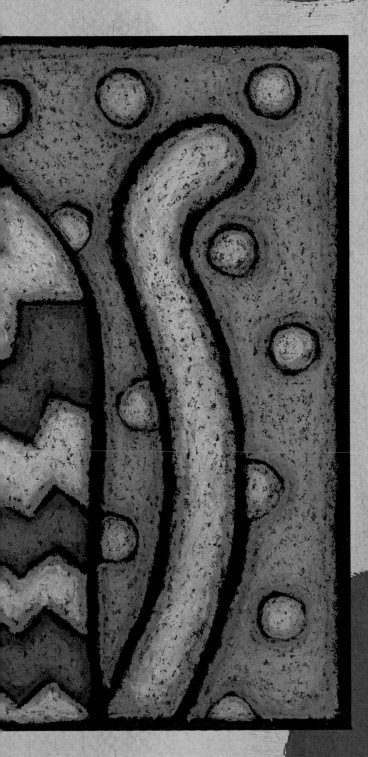

One day a cat decided to count how many legs it had. "Let's see, I have two front legs, two back legs, two left legs, and two right legs. How many is that? Hmm, far too many for me to count in my head. . . . I'll draw lines." And the cat began to draw lines for its back legs and left legs. The other cats watched with interest. "What are you staring at? Help me count!" said the cat mathematician angrily.

So they all began to draw lines for their front legs, back legs, left legs, and right legs. But because none of them managed to count accurately, they're still drawing lines. And people think they are sharpening their claws.

People think they are sharpening their claws, but really they are shredding the couch or the rug because they don't like it.

Cats scratch different surfaces to mark their territory. They also do it to get rid of the old upper layer of their claws. They prefer to sharpen their claws on a tree trunk or piece of wood. In an apartment they tend to choose an armchair, a couch, or a rug.

Why do cats lick their

fur?

 Listen to this story. A family of giants had a cat that was crazy about chocolate. So crazy that one day it jumped into a cauldron full of melted chocolate that the mother giantess intended to use as cake frosting. The giantess pulled the cat out by the tail and, shrieking, drove it out of the kitchen.

"A self-propelled chocolate lollipop!" yelled the giant children enthusiastically when they saw the chocolate-covered cat run out the door with its tail raised. They had already begun to lick their lips and reach out toward the cat, but to their disappointment it quickly licked its own fur clean and went to sleep behind the stove.

 Tell that fairy tale to someone else! Cats lick themselves so they don't have to lick anyone else.

Like dogs, cats do not cool down by sweating, but only by breathing through their mouths. When it is hot, cats lick themselves to cool down. They also remove dirt from their fur by licking. In doing so, they swallow the hairs that collect on their rough tongue. They cough these hairs out as hair balls.

Why do cats' eyes glow

in the dark?

One day the cats and the moles had a bet to determine who could stare at the sun the longest. The cats, being cunning, quickly closed their eyes, while the moles stared at the sun so long that it burned their eyes. From that time onward moles are blind and cats' eyes, because of their short look at the sun, glow in the dark.

Oh, dear me, what nonsense! In reality, cats warm themselves in the sun or on the stove so much during the day that the straw in their heads catches fire, and at night this burning straw shines through their eyes.

I thought fireflies had flown into their eyes.

In the dark, cats' pupils (the black circle in the middle of your eye) widen a lot. This means that their eyes can absorb a lot more light than our eyes or dogs' eyes. We see cats' eyes shining because the light is reflecting from the back of their eyes.

Why do cats bury their

poo?

Long ago, cats did not bury their poo but rather displayed it like a work of art. "What are you trying to say with that?" asked the hedgehog who came across one such sculpture and held his nose. Nor was it clear to the other animals. "Why don't you bury your works of art, and in a thousand or more years your clever descendants can deal with them!" they said to the cats. "You're not smart enough to understand what we're trying to say," said the cats. "We'll bury our works of art and let them be found by someone who appreciates them!"

And still today cats bury their poo because nobody knows how to value their art.

What art?! Their poo smells so bad that they would pass out if they didn't bury it!

Wild cats bury their poo so that it does not attract parasites and so that the smell does not disturb the stronger members of their family. For domestic cats, their owners represent the stronger members of their family.

Why do some cats imitate

rying babies?

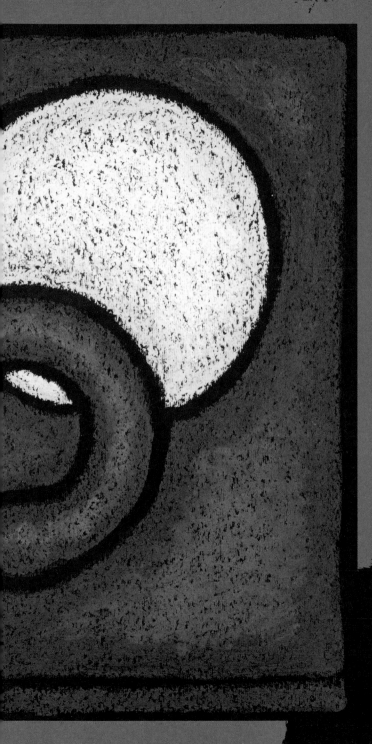

 There's a story about this! Once there lived a witch who couldn't stand the sound of crying babies. So she decided to change every baby she saw into a cat. But the babies she changed into cats gathered beneath the witch's window every night and cried without stopping. *Let the devil take them*, thought the witch. She drank one of her most disgusting potions to calm her nerves and cast a spell to change the cats back into babies. "That's it!" cried a cat. "If you cry, you'll change into a person!" So all the cats started to imitate crying babies. The witch, cursing loudly, flew off somewhere on her broom, and even today cats are still convinced that if they cry they can change into people.

 They're not imitating babies! They're rehearsing an opera!

The sounds that cats sometimes make under our windows at night are not imitations of a baby's crying but the "roaring" that tomcats make to frighten off their opponents in the fight for a queen cat. Queen (female) cats also sometimes give out a "roar" when they're defending their kittens or their territory.

Why do cats hiss?

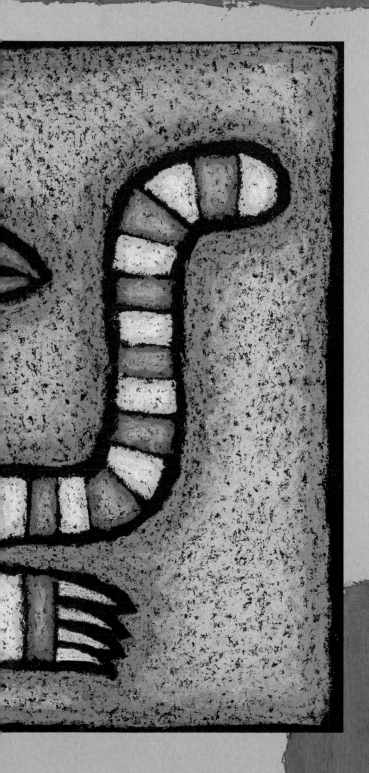

There was a family who had a cat that had everything. They treated him like a king. Then the children decided they wanted a polecat as well. But when the polecat came to live in the house, their cat went crazy. "I'm not sharing this house with anyone!" the cat yelled. "Least of all with some bad-tempered creature that wanders around the house as if it had a firecracker up its bottom!" "I'll show you what kind of firecracker I have!" said the polecat with a big fart. The cat almost threw himself off the windowsill, where it was sunbathing. "You just wait," yowled the cat. "I'll give you such a fart that it will stick you to the ceiling!" It inflated its stomach, but as the fart did not work, all the smelly air came out through its mouth—*hiss.* "Not bad!" said the polecat. "Even I don't know how to do that!" Since that time, the polecat and the cat were friends, and the cat, pleased with its invention, taught all its offspring how to hiss.

I thought they were drying their nail polish!

Cats hiss whenever they feel threatened. They do it to warn a person or animal not to get too close or else an unpleasant surprise awaits the individual—being torn apart by teeth and claws. Other warning signs include growling, raised fur, and flattened ears.

Why do cats pee on

doors?

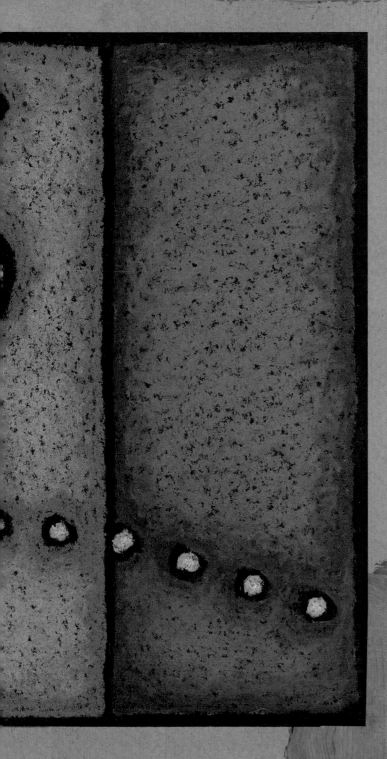

I've got this one! A rich widower had a cat that lived very well until . . . until the widower met a friendly lady and married her. As soon as the lady moved into the widower's house, she became a terrible grouch. "I don't like this dress, this jewelry is too cheap, and your cat smells horrible. I'm allergic to cat hair. We should get rid of it!" she shrieked. The widower tried his best to satisfy her whims, but he could not bring himself to get rid of the cat. "Either the cat goes or I do!" yelled the woman, and the widower had no choice but to take the cat out of the house. The cat lifted its tail high, trembling with rage, and peed on the closed front door. "I'm going to do it every day until she moves out," the cat puffed. And that is exactly what happened.

Really? A bedtime story! Cats do this because they can't tell the difference between a door and a toilet.

Cats mark their territory by peeing on different vertical surfaces. They are solitary animals, so they don't want another cat in their territory. Both tomcats and queens do this. They do it particularly when there are other cats or four-legged animals in the neighborhood.

Why are cats afraid of

There is an old story about a witch who had a cat that did nothing but sleep all day on the stove and sharpen its claws on the witch's most beautiful and expensive rug. "If I see you scratching my rug once more, I'll change you into a frog!" the witch grumbled. Then one day when the cat did it again, she grabbed a pan of water and poured it over the cat. "Ha! Ha! Ha! One, two, three—now you're a frog! At least frogs don't have claws to ruin my rugs." The cat turned green, let out a croak, and, before it turned into a frog, shook the water off its fur. From that day on the witch fibbed that she had a frog at home. All the other cats that heard about this unhappy cat made sure that they stayed well away from water.

Ha! They're afraid of water because they're dirty pigs and don't want to wash!

Wild cats in warm countries like to cool down in water. They know how to swim and some even catch fish. But wild cats in cold countries avoid water because they could catch a cold. Even among domestic cats there are some that like water, but for some the idea of having water poured on them is a nightmare.